from cage to sky

learning to trust these wings of mine

janelle fettes

blissful books

To my biggest cheerleaders.

The ones who have been there every step of the way in making this life-long dream of mine come true. You listened, you encouraged, and you supported me.

Keith, Brynn and Kaybree, you are my greatest inspirations in this life. Your love keeps me going, and your existence gives me purpose.

We are better together.

I love us.

preface

"From Cage to Sky" in no way means I've reached some enlightened end point, but rather have entered a new phase of my journey, free from many of the things that kept me caged for years. One where I've accepted my humanness, and have finally begun to see my own worth. One in which I'm practicing the arts of surrender and faith, and trusting that when I spread my wings, they will carry me.

Thank you for witnessing my journey.

Thank you for supporting my vulnerability.

Thank you for accepting the invitation to reflect upon your own.

Inside I'm dying.
They all think I'm out flying,
but my wings won't spread far enough for me.

- Kaybree Fettes, age 8

This is me.
Each moment I'm unfolding.

Life blurred by the dark, gloomy lens of my past.
Trapped inside old memories and beliefs, I can't seem to escape.
Doors locked, windows rolled up tight - tears streaking down the glass.
Banging with both fists, screaming, hoping someone will rescue me.
Is anyone out there?

Stumbling.
Out of control.
Green with envy, red with rage.
Hurt spiraling, life draining.
Crumbling.

Inside thunder shakes,
roaring with intensity.
My fragile heart breaks.

I can feel it rising,
the dark tar I know as fear.
Climbing through my body,
paralyzing me right here.

Seeping into every crevice,
every corner – body, mind.
Washing out every glimmer
of peace and light left behind.

Feeling like I'm sinking,
I can't breathe, my throat's closed.
Tears cascading out of nowhere,
down my cheeks like a ghost.

Cry
to connect
to feel
to release
to let go
to save yourself from drowning.

Her little body curled into a fetal position – her safe space.
Shutting out the world around her, she rests her head on a pillow of dreams.
A blanket of hope drapes around her tiny shoulders.
She strokes her fear and soothes the tremble within her heart.
Blocking out the surrounding noise, she hums herself to sleep.

Praying
for a miracle,
for the chaos to end.
That you'd say no to drinking buddies,
and choose us instead.

Praying
for a life
that feels calm and safe.
For my mind to quit worrying.
For my heart not to race.

Praying
each day
for as long as I recall,
for you to just stay sober,
and be there for us all.

After years of praying,
my miracle took place.
And with it, deep gratitude,
and strength in my faith.

What if the mess you were born into,
the constant disorder,
your untidy humanness,
was all beautiful chaos?
And rather than perfecting and rejecting,
you embraced it,
and danced amongst the shambles?

She looked and longed for love and approval.
In partners.
In friends.
In praise and recognition.

But it never felt enough.
She never felt enough.

It couldn't be found "out there."
It had always been within.

Years spent counting, tracking, weighing.
Looking in the mirror through eyes of disgust, resentment, criticism.
Forcing and pushing, but never measuring up.
Disciplined. Regimented. Completely disconnected
from my body, my desires, my true self.

Rules came before intuition.
Rigidity replaced flexibility.
Pressure erased ease.

Caged, imprisoned, contained.
Behind bars I'd built myself.

Am I enough?
Do I measure up?

Hair thick,
Eyes bright,
Body thin,
Wrinkles light.

Am I enough?
Do I measure up?

Mind sharp,
Fashion chic,
Brows shaped,
Voice meek.

Am I enough?
Do I measure up?

Skin smooth,
Complexion clear,
Bank account full,
A 6-figure career.

Am I enough?
Do I measure up?

Will these words always haunt me?
Even with boxes ticked?
Will I EVER be enough?
Adored?
Loved?
Perfect?

Running.
Heart pounding,
sweat dripping,
anger rising.

Running.
Voices taunting,
pace increasing,
pain stabbing.

Running.
No slowing,
no stopping,
no feeling.

Running.
Away
from
it all.

A schedule jam-packed,
racing here, rushing there.
Full speed ahead,
not a moment to spare.

A body so drained,
feeling lifeless and weak.
Hardly able to function,
barely wanting to speak.

A mind so scattered,
attention won't stay.
Mental clarity gone,
nothing to say.

A heart so unsettled,
anxious and aching.
Emotions so powerful,
my Soul's suffocating.

I've spread myself out,
much too far, much too thin.
Burnt out, exhausted,
empty within.

All the pressures, the expectations, the guilt, the doubts,
swirl around me,
pushing me
closer
and
closer
to the edge
of the cliff.

I'm drained of the energy it would take to resist.

I let things slide.
I let myself slide.

Hanging
by a thread.
Waiting for one last shove
to send me spiraling
down into the darkness below.

Falling.
Flailing.
Crashing.

Into stillness.
Silence.
The unknown.

No room for error,
no space for mistakes.
Rigid, controlling,
searching for an escape.

The armor shatters, crumbles, falls into pieces.
I step over the rubble.
My soul releases.

My self-doubt shows up as excuses,
as sabotage, envy and fear.
It shows up as an imposter,
a fake who shouldn't be here.

It shows up as criticisms, and bullies in my head.
It tries hard to silence me. It tries to stop me dead.

But I pause and remind myself, I'm needed, and I'm brave.
That progress, and the process, are the experiences I'll save.

That I can't mess this up, that failure is a lie.
That I'll learn from it all - the joy, pain and strife.

Self-doubt loses its power,
when we detach and enjoy the ride.
When we realize our own power,
to quiet the voices in our minds.

Overwhelm, panic, resentment,
they're closing in on me.
I'm left without space.
I need room to breathe.

What will I do,
with the signs I'm being given?
Plaster a smile?
Keep them all hidden?

I won't cover them with bandages.
I'll no longer numb or hide.
I'll open the wound up.
I'll stick my hand inside.
I'll find the embedded thorn,
that's causing my distress.
I'll lie in the discomfort.
I'll rest in the mess.
And whenever it's time,
I'll remove the offending sliver.
I'll scream and cry in pain.
I'll shake. I'll quiver.
And slowly, surely, lovingly,
my wound will begin to heal.
I'll catch my breath again,
with room to move, space to feel.

What if all the fear disappeared,
opinions of others didn't matter,
there was no such thing as failure,
attachments began to shatter.

I'd be more adventurous,
I'd feel much more brave,
steps forward less shaky,
decisions easily made.

I'd live from my heart,
my life more aligned,
I'd trust my inner compass,
I'd get out of my mind.

My worries would be little,
my faith would be strong,
my shoulders would feel lighter,
my list of gratitude long.

Lay down your worries.
Gently step over your fears.
Wrap yourself in faith and love.
Rest and breathe here.

We've gotten so good at covering up our true selves.

We drink alcohol to be more outgoing and fun.

We use camera filters to be more attractive and desirable.

We stay at jobs we hate to prove our success.

We busy ourselves to avoid how we really feel.

We plaster a smile to show that everything is "great!"

What would happen if we allowed our true selves to be seen?!

Perhaps we would attract the people, places and things that are actually meant for us.

That align with who we really are.

Perhaps we would finally belong, rather than trying to fit in.

Sometimes we don't realize we need a break until we take one.

Sometimes we don't admit we need help until it's given.

Sometimes we don't appreciate what we have until it's gone.

Lonely and sullen,
lost and alone,
love is a beacon,
guiding me home.

Home to the place,
I know deep inside,
the place where my soul,
tenderly resides.

A love like no other,
a connection so deep,
the one with myself,
the home that I keep.

I had forgotten.

What true joy and contentment felt like.

How important strong, open relationships are.

How music speaks to my soul, and dancing to my body.

How much I need ease and spaciousness.
Space for me. For the people I love. For the things that light me up.

And in an instant, I remembered it all, and began to live again.

Set goals - specific, measurable, attainable, realistic, with a date. Work hard. Don't give up. Keep going. No excuses.

I did life like this for years. It was exhausting. Pushing to achieve, perform, level up. To earn more, be better, obtain a title. Eventually I reached a point where I couldn't do it anymore. When overwhelm led to burn out, to anxiety, then mild depression, I knew there had to be another way. In order to not only survive, but reclaim my joy, passion, and peace, I had to stop pushing.

I wasn't giving up, I was giving myself a chance.

We don't have to live life in the way we've been told we do. We don't have to constantly strive to climb higher or get the "next best thing" - the "better" body, the higher income, the material possessions, the medals and awards, the outer praise.

We can do anything we choose, but we don't have to do anything we haven't.
No one gets to decide for us.

When I was forced to slow down, I looked at my life and realized I already had what I had been chasing...I just hadn't taken the time to notice. I had been too busy striving for "more."

Maybe more is better. Maybe less is more.
I want less that feels like more.

I still remember the day I ran a marathon. I was smiling, but it was not happiness that I was feeling. I was running, but the joy had been lost long before. I was crossing a goal off my list, but for all the wrong reasons.

When I look back at photos, I am flooded with memories of unworthiness and pain. Of proving and numbing. And all I want to do is hug myself and say all the things I wish I'd been told then.

Obviously I can't go back, and this time in my life was as important as any. It was part of my journey and who I am today. The healing has been painful and messy; unraveling years of hiding, pretending and forcing has felt unbearable at times. And yet, I trust the unfolding.

Each year I shed layer upon layer. And as I do, I fall more in love with the present version of myself. I am more compassionate and understanding with her than I've ever been. I'm realizing that I was not alone in my suffering all these years like I thought I was, nor am I now. I'm not the only one who has hidden her pain beneath a smile.

It's time we stop hiding and start talking. It's time we allow our stories to connect and heal us. It's time we hold each other's hands as we walk along this journey called life.

No pain, no gain.
Tough it out.
Push through.

Loud.
Exhausting.

Is this the way for you?

There's a way that is gentler.
Quieter.
Lighter.

A way that's all yours – where you are the writer.

Slow down. Simplify. Create. Soften.
Offer grace and compassion.
Check in often.

Perhaps this is the way, that your Soul's been seeking.
Sending whispers, signs, nudges and feelings.

Guiding you back to the comfort within,
to the person you are, and have always been.

She's still in there,
that girl with the twinkle in her eye.
The spontaneous one, who loves a surprise.

She's still in there,
that girl who dances and sings.
The one who's carefree, doesn't worry about things.

She's still in there,
that girl who imagines and dreams.
The one who's a fairy or angel, it seems.

She's still in there,
that girl who shimmers and shines.
The one whose magic lives deep inside.

She's still in there.
She's hoping,
to come out and play.
Will you join her?
Embrace her?
Let HER lead the way?

E - evoking
M - magic
E - expelling
R - rigidity
G - growing
E - empowered
N - nurturing
C - creativity
E - expanding

Unbutton the blouse of pressure,
unzip the coat of force,
unravel the stories you've told yourself,
and step onto a whole new course.

What if we put as much energy into loving ourselves as we do into wishing we were different?

This year...

I hope you take time to slow down.

I hope you soak in life's simple joys.

I hope you notice and celebrate all the good in your life.

I hope you remember to play and laugh, and not take life so seriously.

I hope you breathe deeply, and know what a great privilege it is to do so.

I hope you forgive, both others and yourself.

I hope you believe in miracles, and expect them.

I hope you dance.

I hope you love with all your heart...especially yourself.

- a message for the New Year

Let beginnings feel light with hope,
rather than heavy with pressure and expectation.
Let them be celebratory, rather than shameful.
Let them feel expansive, open and flowing,
rather than constrictive, closed off and rigid.

I didn't realize I was half holding my breath for half my life, until I fully exhaled.

We live in a world of instant gratification. Of impatience. Of more is better, and quicker is best.

But what about the things that take time?

To unravel.
To grow.
To transform.

The things that can't be rushed?

Like our hopes. Our dreams. Our authentic selves.

Good things take time.
Give yourself time.

When my loved ones are going through difficult times and get down, I wish they could see themselves how I see them. I wish they could see their beauty, their light and their gifts - all the things that make them who they are. I wish they could feel what I do when I look into their eyes or watch them in their essence.

If I wish this for them, I know someone else is wishing it for me. Someone else sees me in a light that I don't see myself. Someone else feels my warmth and wishes I could feel it too.

Always.

Never.

Is there such a thing in life?! Can we know with such conviction before the present moment arrives?!

We love certainty as humans. We love to know ahead, and we love to have a plan. But what if we took each moment, and ourselves, as is... with curiosity and interest? What if we lived life as an adventure, exploring ourselves as mysteries never to be fully solved?!

There'll be ups and downs.
Redirections along the way.
The challenge is to accept it all –
the black, the white, the grey.

To trust in a higher power,
to surrender to her will,
to breathe through the discomfort,
to know, by being still.

The more we move with life,
relaxing into the flow,
the less painful it will feel,
and the more that we will grow.

But if we choose to fight,
attempting to control,
life will feel a whole lot tougher -
mind, body, spirit, soul.

Life's full of ups and downs.
Light and dark in every day.
The challenge is to allow,
and get out of our own way.

I know I wouldn't have chosen the discomfort or the struggle that I've been through in my life. At times, it has hurt like hell.

I wouldn't have chosen heart break. I wouldn't have chosen rejection. I wouldn't have chosen exhaustion or depletion.

Our soul knows that if it was left to us, we wouldn't choose the path of pain; even if we know it'll make us stronger, more aware, more conscious, softer, more grateful.

A higher power puts things in our lives to grow us in ways that we couldn't without the experience. Someone else needs to be in charge because she can see the blossoming, the healing, the other side. She sees it all and knows it'll be worth it. We can only see what's right before us, and when it's scary or painful, we would choose to turn and run.

The greatest fear of my life had come true – more than once.

I had been rejected, chosen over, left alone, shown I was "not enough."
Only after the heartbreak and pain eased, could I see that what I'd been
trying my hardest to protect myself from, was exactly what I needed to
move forward and heal.

The darkness,
the stillness,
the silence,
the emptiness,
needn't be feared.
For within them,
is the chance to know your soul.

"If I don't push myself, I'll get complacent and stuck."

"If I don't have rules, I'll let myself get away with everything."

"If I rest when I want to, I'll never get anything DONE!"

"If I let myself eat whatever I want, I'll never stop."

These were the constant voices in my head for years. Some of them still show up at times. But when they do, I remind myself that life doesn't have to feel pressured or forceful in order to be successful and amazing. There IS another way. There IS a gentler way. There IS a more compassionate way. One in which we begin trusting ourselves, quieting the inner voices, and healing the deep stuff underneath. It begins with awareness - of our mind chatter, our conditioned beliefs, and our fears driving all the pressure.

Keep it all together.
Be positive, upbeat.
Nothing else welcome.
Suppress if you need.
So you can be perfect -
the flower in a patch of weeds.
It's time to let your humanness out.
To let all of you free.

Both the light and the dark are needed,
but let's not unpack our bags in the dark.

I spent the majority of my life trying to "make something of myself," because it's what I'd learned I was "supposed to do." I was "smart, with drive and dedication" (aka a perfectionist with several disorders). I had "so much going for me." I "could do anything!" And I could, but I never once checked in with what I wanted outside of society and everyone-around-me's ideas and desires for me. I just chameleoned into what I thought was "right, good, and successful." It was exhausting. It was so far from my deep core values and truth, that I constantly felt out of place and not enough.

If you've got big, lofty goals that feel exciting and uplifting for you, great! If you're peaceful and content with what society would deem "small," also great! We put so much pressure on ourselves and our kids to "do big things" - expectations that may very well not be what brings out the best in us or them.

To each their own. Truly.

I can tell you, my life right now at age 40, looks nothing like I imagined it would. But it looks a lot like what I dreamt of as a little girl, before I was redirected by society and well-wishing people.

No one is better or worse based on a job title or a list of accomplishments. Be proud and don't downplay the things that light you up, but also don't look down on others who are content with simple, quiet and slow. The world needs everyone to make it go 'round. Can we start embracing all roles, all jobs, all PEOPLE, without acting as though everyone wants what we want? As though everyone's goal in life is the same? I challenge us all to start...and then notice how much more loving of a place the world is. After all, isn't that the "big thing" more than anything else - to love and be loved?

Looking back over my life, I can see now
that each thing I clung to,
each thing I believed I couldn't live without,
slipped through my fingers.
Perhaps to teach me the art of non-attachment.
To teach me how very little I actually need.
How to loosen my grip.
How to flow with life.
How to trust in the journey.
To help me understand that what's meant for me will stay.

I was called to the place where natural things bloom,
without force or a human hand.
Where life flows full circle,
I was called to this land.

Hundreds of miles walked,
thousands of tears shed.
A return to myself,
with strength to begin again.

- the healing power of the prairie hills

I'm no longer able to tolerate mechanical or robotic.

For so long I moved my body rigidly - in ways that were prescribed to me, or were supposed to change my body into something "worthy." There was no connection. No compassion. No depth. I was on autopilot.

When I experienced what it felt like to MOVE my body and CONNECT with her, exercise regimes, meal plans and itineraries began to feel like cages. All the years of being passionate about wellness, and I had been missing out on the soul.

Now I move, eat and live to connect with myself and my body on a deeper level. I want to know how I feel, what I need and the ways in which I can best serve and care for this vessel of mine. I want to experience life from the inside out - to sense, to feel, to be, without rules or mechanics.

And THAT feels so much truer and more purposeful for me. No more body manipulation. No more "going through the motions". No more of anything that doesn't feel loving, joyful and compassionate.

Health is not all or nothing.

Wellness is not strict or rigid.

Taking care of ourselves means being flexible and flowing - adapting as we go, checking in with ourselves often. This is how we build self-trust. This is how we improve our health and well-being.

It's not one size fits all. It's finding what fits YOU, here and now.

Intuitive eating liberates.

It means we can fully live and enjoy, because we're no longer preoccupied with food.

We're able to cherish the moments that matter, and cultivate connections that count.

It's saying yes to Friday night pizza with our families, and tasting the cake our kids proudly baked.

It's savoring holiday meals that only come once a year.

It's eating and living in the moment, rather than having to plan ahead.

It's choosing what sounds, looks and smells good, without guilt or stress.

It's choosing what we really want, and passing when it doesn't make our mouths water.

It's creating memories that involve food, and ones that don't.

It's dropping the guilt, knowing that food and eating are part of the human experience.

It's rebelling against diet culture, and letting the weight loss and beauty industries know we've had enough.

It's a process.

It's not an overnight shift, nor an easy one. But we can all learn food freedom.

And our lives will be so much richer when we do.

Never underestimate the wisdom and knowledge you've acquired from living in your body.

YOU are the most knowledgeable expert on YOU. Don't slough off what you know about yourself: what feels good, what doesn't, what works, what doesn't. No one else knows your body like you do. After all, you've been living in it for years.

We give away so much of our power to the "professionals" and "experts." And thankfully, they offer so much. But we forget to check in with ourselves as the leading expert. We are the only ones who have been IN our bodies. We are the only ones who know how things feel from the INSIDE OUT.

How do I love me?
Let me count the ways...

This strong and healthy body,
moves me through the days.

This mind that is sharp,
and oh, so very wise,
will continue to keep learning,
until the day I die.

This heart offers kindness,
to everyone I meet,
forgives and moves on,
spreading love with every beat.

The parts that I struggle
to accept, embrace and love,
about which I pray for guidance,
from within me, and above.

So many things to love,
if I only choose to see,
I'm incredible, miraculous,
simply, because I'm me.

I AM BLESSED.
In the times when my body aches and my mind is less than optimistic.

When my house is a disaster and the people in it can't seem to get along.

When I feel stuck, unmotivated and "lazy."

When nothing seems to be going my way.

I AM BLESSED.
With a body that serves me in a million ways each day, without asking for much in return.

I AM BLESSED.
With a warm place to call home, shared with people who forgive and love unconditionally.

I AM BLESSED.
With time and space to rest, relax and honor my needs.

I AM BLESSED.
With Divinity - a Higher Power that has a plan for me.

Even in times of "struggle."
I AM BLESSED.
May I be reminded.
May I be guided.
May I live with gratitude in my heart, and abundance in my mind.

Mid-life.

It's not a crisis, but a beautiful unfolding - an awakening.

A discovery of what's truly important and meaningful.

A reflection on how we've been living life thus far and how it feels inside.

An affirmation or a redirection.

She would continuously reassure me, "It's divinely orchestrated. No matter what you choose nor what you do, you can't mess this up."

- life wisdom given to me from one of my greatest coaches

Grief, I've learned, is not reserved for times of death, but also for loss,
redirections, and everyday disappointments.
We grieve the death of
dreams,
visions,
relationships,
passion, excitement, anticipated outcomes,
and old versions of ourselves.

I took my sorrow to the river,
expecting I might drown.
But instead, I floated with it,
gliding up-stream and down.

When was the last time you checked in with your heart?
Gave your aching attention, comfort, love and tenderness?

The less I fight my worry, the less anxious I become.

Even when big "disasters" and life changing catastrophes aren't happening in our lives, it can still feel difficult.

Even when life seems pretty damn amazing, we can still feel sad and not know why.

Even when we are surrounded by amazing people, we can still feel lonely.

Our feelings are real. They are valid. And they deserve love and compassion.

Every trigger.
Every reaction.

An opportunity.

For curiosity.
Expansion.
Compassion.

How often do we complain and talk about this or that, which doesn't affect us or our lives?

What if instead we used our time and energy on our own lives, not someone else's? What if we stayed focused on what we can do, not on what we can't? What if we let others live their lives their way, and we lived ours in our way - in peace. It might not be easy to start, because habits take time and practice to reroute, but we can keep steering ourselves back into our own lane.

Compassion begins when we focus on our similarities and connection to others more than on our differences and separation. When we aim to see ourselves in others, and others within ourselves.

We see a mother being short with her child, and instead of judging, we remember when just the other day we lost our patience too.
We notice an acquaintance avoid our gaze and quickly step out of the store, and we recall all the times when we didn't feel like engaging in small talk either.
We are about to yell at our son/daughter for spilling food on the freshly washed floors, and we remember that we too make mistakes.

With each return to love,
with each pause to remember that we've all felt sadness, anger, hurt,
with each moment of putting ourselves in others' shoes,
we take a step into compassionate living,
and we move toward world peace.

Move your body to
Energize
Strengthen
Shift
Release
Uplift

Get still to
Reconnect
Ground
Breathe
Listen
Be

If we don't move, we stay stuck.
If we don't stop, we keep spinning.

Moving my body still lifts me up, but the way I move has transformed.

Eating delicious food still brings me joy, but my intentions have evolved.

Self-care is still a priority, but the way I care for myself has shifted.

Setting boundaries is necessary, but having strict rules is not.

May we be open to change.
May we allow our evolution and our renewal.
May we embrace our ever-evolving selves.

When your mind starts to spin,
when your heart starts to race,
when the world feels unpredictable,
and the ground seems to shake...

Take a moment to pause,
to notice what's inside.
Breathe.
Be present.
Let be.
Simplify.

"Please help them choose me."
"Please help our relationship work out."
"Please help me to be accepted."
"Please don't let this happen.
"Please make that happen."

I've prayed these words and many more along the same lines throughout my life. I've prayed for people to stay, for things to go "my way," for my life to look the way I had envisioned.

And sometimes they did. Sometimes I got exactly what I prayed for. But I didn't feel the way I thought I would.

Other times things went very differently than I had hoped, and it turned out to be the greatest blessing of my life.

We don't always know what's best for us, or how things will feel when we get them. It's why it's so important to trust fully and deeply in a power higher than our minds and our own control. It's why our goals need space and flexibility. It's why our prayers need less specificity and more faith.

Now, my prayers sound more like:
"Please help things work out for the best of everyone."
"Please show me the next best step."
"Please give me strength to get through this."
"Please guide me."

Today, I invite you to notice where you may be holding on tightly to a specific outcome, and how you could loosen your grip and trust more fully.

Don't pray for outcomes,
pray for strength to overcome.

-wisdom from a dear friend

Often, the things we fear the most, are the things that hold with them, the highest freedom.

Often, the experiences we resist the most, are the ones that will bring us the greatest growth.

Often, the people we shrink and cower around, are meant to teach us the most about ourselves.

With each chance I take,
with each mistake I make,
I learn and I grow.

Reading through old journals reminds me that even when it doesn't feel like I've been growing and changing, I have.

I'm reminded that what hurts so badly right now, will evolve into a beautiful life experience and lesson.

I'm reminded that things I don't think I'll ever heal from, will eventually feel lighter.

I'm reminded that if I put in the work, and have the courage to "go there," my past will lose its power over me.

I'm reminded how resilient, strong, courageous, and committed I am.

I'm reminded that life changes for our highest good, and even if we can't see it in the moment, we will when we look back.

Success is not in things.
It's not in outcomes.
It's not "out there."

Success is inside.
It's in how you see yourself.
It's in how you speak to yourself.
It's in how you feel.
It's in how you treat others.
It's in how you live your life, regardless of what you do or don't have.

Success is knowing who you are, believing in yourself, and following what you know is right for YOU.

What success looks like on the outside doesn't matter compared to how it feels on the inside.

The outer world is a reflection of our inner world. So naturally, the best way to start healing the planet, is to begin healing ourselves.

Healing:
releasing the heavy,
holding onto the light,
knowing the difference,
deep down inside.

What feels dreadful and heavy to one, feels purposeful and light to another. And one day, you may wake up and find that what used to feel good for you, no longer does.

When someone shares her story, it isn't meant to become YOUR truth - but sometimes it will resonate deeply. Follow the resonation, even if you don't know why.

Take what feels good, and leave the rest...

If you were to live your life with your eyes and ears closed, not able to see or hear others' reactions, what would you choose?

What if we focused on connecting with ourselves as much as we focused on connecting with others?

When our primary intention is to feel good, without attachments or expectations, we naturally align with our best self. From this place, our health, relationships, careers, life purpose – our entire lives – fall into place.

One day, after years of living in restriction and rigidity, I "woke up" and asked myself, "Where did I get these rules that I've held to so firmly for years?!"

The numbers I was obsessed with, the goals that I was killing myself to achieve...whose rules were these?!

When we begin to question why we are doing the things we do, we open up space for immense awareness and healing.

When we question and allow for honest answers to surface, we may realize that the life we are living is not our own.

Our real, authentic selves don't need rules, rigidity or restriction. We need compassion, flexibility and freedom to follow the wisdom of our hearts, souls, and bodies.

If we are doing things for the sake of "health," but the things are making us miserable, is that healthy?

If we're following the books and the guides, but it's sucking the joy from our lives, is that healthy?

If we are not being curious and exploring what's right for our own bodies, minds and spirits, are we truly on the path to health and wellness?

Body size and appearance were obsessions of mine for years. How I looked on the outside was my main priority -my gauge for success.

I did everything I could to be thin, toned, "beautiful" and "perfect." I ate only certain foods. I engaged in grueling exercise regimens. I tried to follow the fashion trends. And if I "slipped up" in any of these areas, or anyone commented negatively about me, I used it as proof that I wasn't good enough, and as a driving force to punish myself and work even harder.

I had no life outside my pursuit for perfection.
I isolated myself and devoted all of my time and energy to "self-care"...except it was the furthest thing from it. It was self-destruction.

Talk about sucking the joy out of life.

My thinking was disordered.
My habits were disordered.
My whole life was disordered.

I was obsessed.
I was distracted.
I was mentally ill.

Trapped.
Suffering.
Lost.

If you can relate, if you know there is more to life than counting calories, exercising your body to exhaustion and achieving the "perfect" appearance, I'm here to tell you that there absolutely is.

There is a soul inside of you that longs for your attention, your compassion, and your love. A Soul that longs to be seen, heard and understood. A Soul that wants to shine. I hope you choose to trust, know and respect her in this lifetime. And I hope you get to watch your life transform as you do.

Experiment with moving in your body as though it's your first time inside. Explore her parts, her beauty, her personality.

What does it feel like to sink your feet into the Earth? To fill your body with breath? To roll up and down your spine?

Can you feel your heartbeat inside your chest as you move? Can you notice the vibration of breath at the back of your throat as you draw on your strength? Can you sense energy travelling through your mind, body and soul?

Become aware. Connect. Sense. Experience the miracle that is you.

I used to dream of rock-hard abs and a flat stomach. Now I'm after rock solid faith and a life that doesn't feel flat.

I used to believe that the more friends I had, the more fun I'd have and the more desirable I was. Now I realize it's all about resonance and finding the people who feel like home.

I used to think health was just about drinking green smoothies and sweating buckets every single day. Now I believe it's about nourishing the mind, body and soul. It's about checking in often and following the guidance from within.

I used to want "success" for myself and my family, and I still do, but my definition of success has changed.

I used to need the approval of others. Now, I know it's not possible to be liked or accepted by everyone. I'll be for some and not for others.

I'm still me, in fact, I'm rediscovering who that is more and more every day. I'm dropping what no longer feels good inside and going deeper within to uncover what does. I'm living more in the present than I have in a very long time. And I'm realizing that a lot of things I thought were certain, are evolving as I get curious.

We're meant to change. We're meant to grow. We're meant to shift. We're meant to flow.

We know, and our bodies know, when we need movement, and when we need rest.

We know, and our bodies know, when we need more, and when we need less.

We know,
and our bodies know,
if we just slow down and tune in.
If we take the time to reconnect,
and trust ourselves again.

When our physical bodies force us to slow down through ailments or symptoms, we become more mindful. We sense more. We become more aware of the daily blessings we've been taking for granted. Even in the discomfort, when things don't go as we'd like, there are gifts wrapped up inside.

How often we wish to change ourselves or our situation, when it's actually our beliefs and thoughts about it that need shifting.

Sometimes I feel small.
Insignificant.
Left wondering if I truly matter.
If I'm making a difference.

And then I remember,
I wouldn't be here if I didn't.
I wouldn't be here if I wasn't.

What we focus on is what we will see.

When we look for problems, we will find them. When we look for solutions, they will come.

When we look for people's flaws and downfalls, they will show themselves. When we look for their best, it will be there too.

When we look for darkness, it will surround us. When we look for the light, it will shine brightly.

What are you looking for? Where are you placing your focus? Because whatever it is, I can guarantee you, you'll find more of it.

Is it time to readjust your lens?

"She's so this. He's so that. I wish they'd..." And then I remember, it's not my life, that's not my path. I continuously and compassionately bring myself back into my own lane.

I focus on MY path - my long, winding, ever-changing path. Without needing to explain or justify why I've chosen the one I have. Never having to downplay my experiences. This journey is mine, and I myself am not even sure where it's going to lead. I keep finding what feels good in the now and trusting that I'll be taken where I'm meant to go, meeting the people I'm meant to meet, and having the experiences I'm meant to have along the way.

And then, I allow others to do the same.

No longer trying to tell you what's right,
nor how to live your one precious life.
Allowing you to have your own journey.
Everyone,
including me.

There are a lot of voices and opinions out there, but once we get more in touch with ourselves, they get quieter and quieter, while the knowing in our heart becomes stronger and stronger.

Giving advice is a whole lot easier than taking it.
Saying it is a whole lot easier than living it.

Just because I can, doesn't mean I want to.

Just because I have the skills and knowledge, doesn't mean I'll accept every invitation to use them.

Just because I've given myself permission to eat all foods, doesn't mean my preferences are always the same.

Just because I honor my body's needs and wishes, doesn't mean there's only one way to meet them.

Just because I'm a sensitive and introverted, doesn't mean I never crave adventure or group energy.

Just because some things are black and others are white, doesn't mean I can't choose grey.

In your mind, your schedule, your heart – allow space.
Resist filling each moment of the day.

For so many years I was striving for a purpose - teaching classes, starting committees, leading groups, giving so much, all with the intent of "making a difference." And I know they did. But I also know that all my hustle, going and doing, left me with an inner void. And now I know why. My purpose isn't only in my work and volunteering. It's not always "out there," but most importantly, it's in the connections I make at home and within. It's in the daughters I'm raising. It's in the support I offer my husband. It's in having the time to connect with friends over tea and deep conversation. It's in having a big heart that wants to help others when they need it, sending a surprise in the mail, a homemade meal, or a gift from the heart. It's in the person that I already am and continue to evolve into.

Our purpose can be fulfilled in our careers and jobs, yes, but it doesn't have to. It can also simply be living authentically from our hearts.

The day I stopped racing,
the day I stopped rushing,
the day I stopped striving,
was the day I started living.

I will never forget the year of 2018 – it was such a wild ride of emotions.

Excitement and eagerness in having completed my yoga teacher training.
Anxiety and nervousness about taking on the new role.
Love and passion for the practice.

Overwhelm and exhaustion from taking on too much, too soon.

Guilt and shame for needing to take a step back.
Fear that maybe I would never come back as energetic, vibrant and
enthusiastic as before.

I remained in "recharge, rejuvenate and reset mode" for a long stretch of
time - much longer than I had anticipated, expected or would've liked.
But it taught me that in life we only have so much control - and the rest
we surrender to natural time and order.

If we want to come out of darkness stronger and lighter, if we want the
low times to fulfill their purpose, then we need to let go and TRUST the
process.

I was so grateful to those patiently waiting and supporting me in these
times. For allowing me to nourish, honor and love myself in the best way
I knew how.

I would've loved to be at every event I was invited to that year. I'd have
loved to host more classes and events. I'd have loved to be feeling
motivated and energetic. But it wasn't the time. It was time to just be and
invite simplicity in.

What "time" is it for you right now in your life? Are you honoring and
allowing it, or pushing through to where you think you "should" be?

Nature's seasons change,
as do the seasons of life.
We don't rush nature.

Some days lying on the Earth, feeling the wind on my skin, and the sunshine on my face is the best medicine.

Some days letting tears fall in showers, and finding complete stillness is the release that's needed.

Some days my voice is quiet, my energy is low, and my focus is introspective.

Every day, I am human, riding the waves of life.
Every day, I am worthy of love, care and respect.
And so are you.

Presence - the most important spiritual practice.

When others come to us in chaotic disarray or emotional turmoil, rather than giving our opinion, dismissing their stresses, or trying to solve their problems, what if we were to simply "be" with them? What if we offered love and comfort with no ulterior motive? What if we were able to simply hold space - gentle, loving, warm space?

We could give them the most valuable gifts: unconditional love, compassion and acceptance. Imagine how this gift would feel to receive. No need to pretend or downplay. The freedom to let out whatever needs releasing, knowing that no matter if the other person agrees or not, they'll be there listening, loving and comforting.

What if we also gave this gift to ourselves? Acceptance of where we're at in the moment, without expecting ourselves to be "further ahead." An offer of deep compassion and love to ourselves - without judgment, criticism, rushing, fixing or dismissing.

Imagine.

After all, isn't what we all need and desire most, unconditional love and acceptance? And often, what we fear most, judgment and rejection?

I believe that less is more.
That the little things in life are actually the big things.

That anything ordinary can be extraordinary if we're open to notice.

That love is the answer to every question.

That healing is an inside job.

That success means believing in ourselves and creating a life that feels good on the inside.

That beauty is more about the way we live and treat one other, than it is about outer appearance.

She rarely sees things in black or white,
yet struggles to be in the grey.
Wishes she could take a strong stand,
but knows that isn't her way.

Head over heart,
her mind swirls, trying to decide.
Weighing this way with that,
feeling pressure, to settle and choose a side.

And then her heart whispers,
"You're the bridge between."
And she felt that – deeply,
she felt heard, she felt seen.

Her essence unveiled,
she stands proudly in center.
Arms outstretched,
she draws all together.

Not everyone loves the way we love.

A lot of disappointment can be spared
in not expecting ourselves from others.

When I was younger, I swore I would never marry a cattle rancher nor live on a farm. I remember in my teens and young adulthood thinking I was too selfish to have kids. I remember the feeling of pure exhaustion while pushing myself to run miles and miles every single day, yet still believing running was my passion.

Here I am now, part of a 450+ cattle operation, living tucked away in the rolling hills of the prairies, with my husband and two daughters, enjoying nature walks and yoga, no longer a "runner."

We never know how life will look in the future. We can't possibly predict or control the events that lead us to where we are today. So, rather than holding on so tightly to our future, what if we loosened our grip? Even just a little? What if we found even a tiny bit of trust and faith that things are falling into place? What if we dipped a toe into the waters of surrender?

We don't know what will bring us joy or peace at a different time in our lives. We may not even know right now. Often what we think it is that we want, turns out not bringing the feelings we believed they would. What if instead of trying to figure it all out, we relaxed into the unknown? And prayed for life to unfold for our highest good and the good of all? Because often what we expect, is not what ends up being reality. We could be the happiest in the spaces we thought would make us miserable.

I no longer pray for specific outcomes,
nor things to turn out my way,
but rather the highest good of all,
and inner peace that stays.

How many times have you started something only to get the end result? You push through, "suck it up" and follow the rules, so you can get to the thing at the end that is so enticing. The thing that is going to "change your life forever." Except when it doesn't.

You cringe, battle your way through, get the end "prize," yet don't feel the way you thought you would. You've spent all this time, energy and effort for something that didn't deliver.

What if, instead of going after the "big game changer," you chose to do things in your life NOW that brought you joy? What if, instead of waiting to reach some end goal to celebrate, you decided every moment was worth celebrating? What if, you enjoyed the process of life instead of waiting "until"...?

I challenge you to take your eyes off the "prize" for a moment and focus your attention on the present moment. How can you add more things to your life right now that feel good, with no end-result attached? Rather than setting yourself up for disappointment, set yourself up for joy - not "when," but now.

We push. We force. We want it so badly that we will do "whatever it takes."

But how often do we stop to ask ourselves why it's not working?

Constantly searching for more clarity and answers,
means we're not trusting the process
or the perfection of what comes next.

Faith in your soul.
Hope in your mind.
Love in your heart.

The reason we choose to do something in our lives, may not be the main reason it's happening in our lives. So often we go in with a premeditated picture of what things will be like, how things will go, and what the outcome will be. And sometimes we're disappointed because what we imagined, is not what reality brought. But if we look deeper, below the surface, and beyond our expectations, we see that it was about so much more than we originally intended.

Jobs taken to provide financially, build relationships and social connections. Events attended out of obligation, help realize new hobbies and passions. Places visited as a casual holiday, offer feelings of security and peace.

Every experience offers us something or it wouldn't have come our way. Often, it's bringing more abundance, wisdom, and open doors than we could imagine. Are you open to seeing? Feeling? Realizing?

When life feels unpredictable, remind yourself that it always is. We could plan every detail with clarity and precision, and have the route take a hard left at any time. We could set up all the steps toward the goal, and suddenly the goal doesn't feel like something we want anymore. We could prep and plan and control all we want, but if it's not the path for our greatest growth nor our purpose here, we will be led elsewhere.

We can fight changes, we can curse the redirection, we can try to stop what's happening, or we can flow with it, learn from it, and honor all the feelings along the way.

I hope you FLOAT.

When life feels overwhelming and unbearable,
I hope you take a deep breath and soar with it under your wings.

When your worries are so big, you feel like you might drown,
I hope you glide on top of the water.

When you don't know which way to go and your mind is hazy,
I hope you allow the clouds to carry you.

When your body feels tense, your mind feels full and your soul weary,
I hope you remember to relax, surrender, let go...
and FLOAT.

What's your anchor?

The thing or place that helps you feel the most like you?

That feels true and real, safe and easy.

The thing that no matter what's going on around you, brings you peace in your heart.

The thing that reminds you to slow down and breathe. To take it all in. That reminds you to feel deeply and live for the moment.

What's your anchor?

Motherhood - it's amazing, it's incredible, it's rewarding. And it's frustrating, draining and exhausting. All at the same time. One minute we are patient and understanding, the next short-tempered and judgmental.

While supporting our kids through their struggles, we are also learning self-compassion. It's a whirlwind of heart-felt emotions. And it can be overwhelming. But we're doing it. We're creating memories with our kids. We're learning and growing, as we love each other through it all.

Motherhood - it's miraculous, it's messy, it's heart-wrenching, and it's perfect. It's chaos and bliss all wrapped up in one. And it's not meant to be any other way.

Celebrating every single Mom out there doing your best in each moment. May you judge yourself less and love yourself more.

- not only on Mother's Day, but every day

We can guide and teach our children, but they'll have their own journeys, mistakes and lessons to learn. We don't own our children's problems. They are their own people.

Good parents make mistakes. Good kids make mistakes. And hopefully, we learn from them. We are here to guide and help our children, but we can't control their every action, nor should we try.

- my constant reminder as I parent my teenage daughters

When our cups are empty, we complain, criticize, belittle and lash out. We envy, we gossip, we downplay and we compare. We take all of our frustrations, our anger and our feelings of unworthiness, and we spew it onto those around us. We hold tightly onto things, we compete and we hoard, believing that success and happiness are scarce and only deserved by a few.

When our cups are full, we express gratitude, we compliment, we encourage, we cheer, we celebrate and we lift others up. We rise. We want nothing but the best for ourselves and others, knowing there is an abundance to fill everyone's cup!

Let this be your invitation and your permission to take time each day, each week, each month, and all year, to fill your cup. To engage in practices and activities that make you feel alive, vibrant and purposeful. To do things that light you up.

We change the world by taking care of ourselves first; by filling our own cup, then allowing it to overflow.

All around her the wind howls,
but within her – at her very centre –
quiet calm finds its home.
Her Soul: the eye of the storm.

Someone once told me, "You need to get really clear on what you want in your life." And at first, that didn't sit well with me. I believe we limit ourselves when we have all the details of our lives planned and figured out ahead of time. When we over-plan, we don't leave room for a Higher Power to bring us what we truly need, rather than what we think we do.

Then, my understanding of what she had said shifted. I don't have to get really clear on what my life or dreams will LOOK like, I need to get clear on how they will FEEL. Inside.

We can feel when something is right for us. There's no denying the peaceful, relaxed inner knowing of our lives falling into place – into alignment.

Get still and ask. Be still and know. Not in your mind, but in your heart and soul.

It all started with a question,
"What do you want?"

My mind tossed and turned.
It reached for big, flashy things.

The voice inside threw out criticisms.
How could I not know the answer?!

I recalled things I'd heard and read:
"Dream BIG."
"Don't give up."
"Work hard to achieve."
"It'll take blood, sweat and tears."
"You've got to get really clear."

And then it came. Clarity. But not from my head, from my heart. A
simple knowing.

I want contentment.
I want peace.
I want joy.

I want to feel safe and loved. Light and free.

I want to really be here. In each moment.
I want to live fully.
I want to soak up every drop of life.
I want to feel vibrant and alive – full of enthusiasm and joy!
I want to talk for hours about things that really matter.
I want to sit side by side and not need to say a word.

I want to celebrate this life I've created, and not apologize for it.
I want to be immersed in sunshine, barefoot in the grass, walking
amongst the hills.

I want all things natural and less fake.

I want to shed tears upon tears, and laugh until my belly aches.

I want to be surrounded by, and filled with, love and acceptance.

I want to move my body because I can.

I want to nourish it with good food, and soothe it with hot baths and rest.

I want to go on adventures with my family and explore new things.

I want to be the person my kids come to.

I want to be strong, solid and stable, while being gentle, compassionate and loving.

I want it all. But I don't want to chase any of it. I want to be open to receive.

I want to surrender and trust, knowing that everything meant for me will find its way. It will not pass me by.

THAT. Is what I want.

What do YOU want?!

Awareness is all.
Set the how aside.

The moment when the veil is lifted, and you realize what your "triggers" and uncomfortable moments have been trying to teach you...

The moment you learn the lesson.

In a world of doing, choose being.

In a world that moves so quickly, choose to slow down.

In a world of chasing more, choose contentment.

In a world of blame, choose compassion.

In a world of fear, choose courage.

In a world of screens, choose human connection.

In a world of distraction, choose presence.

In a world of conformity, choose authenticity.

In a world of people-pleasing, choose yourself.

In a world of uncertainty, choose faith.

In a world of comparison, choose collaboration.

In a world of anything and everything, choose that which makes your heart sing.

Remember when you prayed for what you currently have?
When my husband worked and lived away as a drilling rig manager, I
longed to have him here with us. I looked so forward to a time when we
could catch up at the end of the day cuddled together, when we could
have meals as a family, when he could be at our girls' events.
And now this is reality.

I used to dream about being at a place where I was not a slave to my
workouts and bound to eating only certain foods at specific times. I
dreamed of respecting, loving, and trusting my body the way it is. And
now this is reality.

When I began to experience burnout, I ached for a schedule that
included space and time to just be. I wished for my work to flow rather
than constantly feeling bogged down by planning and perfecting. And
now this is reality.

For years I've hoped that I could make a difference. That I would create
what I wish existed. That what I did would matter. That my life would
have an impact.
And now this is reality. It always was, I just didn't see it or believe it
until now.

Remember when you longed for some of the things you currently have?

Even the tiniest thing - the way you wanted to feel inside, the
relationship you wanted to strengthen, the courage you hoped for.
Take a look. I bet you have more than you realize.

Redirect the energy you have tied up in chasing "more," into appreciating what you already have.

Hills that keep on rolling,
for as far as I can see.
Within them – silence, stillness, spaciousness,
and endless amounts of peace.

Lying on the ground,
listening to the sound of my heart beating,
feeling the waves of my breathing,
no longer able to separate myself from Mother Earth.

Before texting for opinions,
phoning for advice,
before reaching out in desperation,
before we look outside...
Can we sit with the discomfort?
Can we look inside?
Can we be still and listen?
Call on our inner guide?

Give yourself permission...

To say yes.
To say no.

To stay.
To go.

To follow your heart.
To follow your soul.

To take a risk.
To stay in comfort zones.

To change your mind.
To stay the same.

To put you first.
To rid the shame.

To not know.
To not have a plan.

To stay silent.
To take a stand.

To rest.
To move.

To be.
To do.

Give yourself permission...to trust yourself and choose.

What is the goal?

To get every step or pose "right"...or to find joy in the movement?

To hold out until we get it all perfected...or to share from the heart, flaws and all?

To constantly strive and search for more and better... or to honor where we are at right now, while continuing to grow?

To follow the crowd and do things because it's "what we do"...or question what it is we really WANT to do?

To change ourselves so we fit in...or be who we are and find where we belong?

To squeeze into society's mold for us...or break free and create our own way?

To please everyone else...
or to live for ourselves?

I'm learning that...

Life is not meant to always be easy and comfortable. Challenge and discomfort are how we learn and grow. If we take away these elements of life, we miss out on some of our greatest growth opportunities.

All parts of ourselves and our lives are interconnected. How we do one thing is how we do the others. And where we lack in one area, we overcompensate in another.

Awareness is key to change. But overthinking causes indecision and paralysis.

Nothing needs to be forced when we're aligned. Things will naturally ebb and flow. The things meant for us will not pass us by.

We are all unique beings, and therefore require different things to thrive. What's right or has worked for one, may not for another.

If we want others to accept us for who we are, we must do the same.

How can we begin accepting ourselves as we are?

How can we begin accepting others as they are?

I don't try to direct others' paths,
I don't try to convince.
I am unable to give directions,
to places I've never been.

How many times do we disregard other people's feelings for our own? How many times do we try to convince others that our story is valid, and theirs is "wrong"? How many times do we attempt to change the way someone else sees us?

Our ego wants everyone to like us, agree with us, and be more like we are. It wants us to be innocent and the hero, every time. But when we are honest and authentic, we know that even when we do what we believe is best, others might not see it that way. They have their own lenses. They have their own history and stories. They have their own values. And all of this and more, frames how they interpret others and their experiences. And the same goes for us.

We don't get to decide how anyone else feels, and they don't get to decide for us either. What we can do, is live with our values at the forefront and check our intentions. And if we know we are living our truth, the rest is up for interpretation, and not something we can control. Our challenge? Make peace within, regardless of how others see us.

I've gotten to a point where I can no longer point outward, without also looking within.

We can shine like soft candle-light, or we can shine like cascading fireworks.
Both are beautiful and breathtaking.
Both are needed in the world.
Why try to be one when you were born to be the other?
Shine as you are.

Some of us are leaders, some helpers.
Some of us entrepreneurs or part of businesses.
Some of us homemakers.

Some of us thrive on busyness and full schedules.
Some need a lot of downtime to function best.
Some of us are a little of each.

Some of us have spent our entire lives trying to be what we're not, trying to fit a mold, trying to be accepted, praised and validated.

Some of us are in the process of unbecoming and remembering who we really are.

Some of us are realizing that what we've been living, and who we've been pretending to be, is not our truth and is no longer possible.

All of us are living life the best way we know how at the time.
We are growing, changing and evolving, maybe without even realizing it.

All of us deserve to do and be what feels best in each moment without guilt, without apology, without feeling inferior.

May we celebrate each of our intricacies, our paths, our authenticity.
May we have the courage to choose a new pace, rhythm or direction any time.
May we support and encourage one another to do so.

May we be as inspired by those choosing less, as we are by those doing more.
May we re-define success on our own terms.
May we embrace who we are and who others are, knowing that the world needs each of us equally, whether "behind the scenes" or "center stage."

May we follow our inner knowing and use our Soul as our compass, rather than society's goals for us.

May we listen to our own voice more than the opinions of others.

May we find peace, love, joy and harmony throughout all stages and phases of our lives.

This life.
It's amazing.
It's challenging.
It's so complex.
As are we.
Can we embrace it all?

This life. It's for living.
This human. She's for loving.

How are you moving through your days - head down, nose to the grindstone?
Or gaze up, taking in all the miracles around you?

Sometimes I slow down, I pause and take note,
of the beauty around me, it's what life's all about.
The melody and laughter from those that I love,
the sun rising and setting, the light shows above.
The feel of the grass between my bare toes,
the smell of fresh rain, that I love the most.
The long, winding driveway that leads to our home,
that reminds me I'm loved and never alone.
My dog so excited to go for a walk,
listening to friends when they need to talk.
This life it's so full, of miracles each day,
that we often rush past as though they'll all stay.
But if taken from us, we'd feel empty, life small,
wishing we'd taken the time, to cherish it all.

Ordinary moments.
Magical moments.
That become one.

Take time to bask in the sparkle.

There are moments that bring so much clarity to our hearts, that we're left wondering how we ever doubted our lives or questioned our purpose.

Drink in those moments. Savor the feeling. They are what life is about. They are what keep us nourished and alive.

When you've acted out of alignment.
When you feel you've lost your way.
When you wish you could go back.
When you don't know what to say.

When your well-meaning advice,
was not received the way you'd hoped.
When you want to make it right.

When you're ready to learn and to grow.

Whenever. Any way.
Anytime. Anywhere.

Love is the answer.

To every question, every prayer.

Healing starts when I'm present.

When I stay rather than run,
when I feel rather than numb.

Peace comes with
acceptance and
unconditional love.

I practice.
I surrender.
To a power up above.

Heart Song

There's a lark that lives in my heart.
It sings sweet songs for me.

Melodies of love,
lyrics of faith,
beautiful rhythms of peace.
There's a lark that sings in my heart.
Soul songs, just for me.

Some days, the world feels like too much. Sometimes, I want to shut it all out and pretend life is just sunshine and rainbows. Some moments, I wish I knew answers I can't possibly know right now, and I wish I could see into the future.

And some days, I can see all that we are being taught and how we are each growing as we navigate through. I want to rewrite news headlines to include all the good that's going on in the world - the little acts of love and support for one another. Some moments, I feel faith so strong within me that I know it's all going to be okay.

I feel it all. And I feel it deeply. I teeter totter from one emotion to the next, from one perspective to another. Things come and go in waves.

This is life as a human being. This is life's school.

Life's full of unforgettable moments,
of amazing, joy-filled days,
of moments we'd rather forget,
days that aren't so great.

We go from the highest of highs, to the lowest of lows,
sometimes within 24 hours,
all part of being human,
rising, falling, finding our power.

Rather than stuffing and hiding,
erasing the joy with the pain,
offer heaps of grace and compassion,
welcome all the wisdom that you'll gain.

Some moments we are "soaring," like we are "on top of the world," as though nothing could get us down.

Others, we are struggling to see the good, to get ourselves off the ground.

We need it all.
We need to land after we fly.
We need the earth, we need the sky.
We need wind beneath our wings, and ground beneath our feet.
There are times to move, and times to be.
We need it all.

Life's a dance,
we learn and we grow.
How, when or why,
we don't always know.

One encounter.
One conversation.
One moment of "yes!"
Can literally change everything.
Perspective. Vibration. Energy.

Passion reignited.
Purpose rekindled.
Reminding us the importance of connection.
With each other.
With our true selves.
With humanity.
With the world.

One word.
One hug.
One smile.
One fleeting moment.
Can be a new beginning.

If we let go of thinking we know best, the best will naturally fall into place.

May I know and feel the vastness of my own light in this lifetime.

You don't have to be so serious,
you're not too old to play,
to throw caution to the wind,
to toss your cares away!

Get your hands dirty,
let the breeze mess your hair,
dance like no one's watching,
let your feet be free and bare!

Do what makes you smile,
giggle 'til your belly aches,
there's nothing quite like laughter,
to forget your mistakes!

Let your shoulders drop,
your jaw tense less,
breathe in ease and joy,
breathe out heaviness.

Say no to all the rules,
and yes to all the fun,
no to being rigid,
yes to staying young!

Let moving joyfully and eating nourishing foods be gifts to your body.

Let engaging in things that light you up be gifts to your soul.

Let rest, stillness, and rejuvenation be gifts to your mind.

Let yourself be loved more than ever.
Let yourself believe you are worthy of it all.

Because if you don't prioritize your peace, who will?

Authenticity or attachment.

We often trade one for the other. We give up what we truly love and the essence of who we are to be accepted, loved, and a part of something.

What if, instead, we found what felt authentic and true for us, and allowed the rest to fall into place? What if, we took care of ourselves and our needs first, trusting that the people and experiences meant for us would arrive?

When faced with the choice
to abandon yourself
or everyone else,
I hope you choose
to stand by you.

Want to love yourself more? Get to know yourself better.

How can we give ourselves more love if we don't know how we need to be loved?

What is love?
What isn't love?
How do you know?

I don't want my schedule
So F U L L
that I don't have time to spare for
calls from my heart and invitations that will fill it.

These Days

It's days that're slow and simple,
some would call lazy or a waste.
These days are my everything,
these days can't be replaced.

No real plan or schedule,
just taking it as it comes.
A little of this, a little of that,
these days - my favorite ones.

Whether surrounded by my people,
or enjoying time alone,
just being and taking it easy,
are the best days I've known.

My Soul calls for space,
in my schedule and my mind.
And it's days like these that satisfy,
that calling from deep inside.

I hope you never lose your love for slow and simple. I hope the world doesn't suck you into its "more is better" illusion. I hope you keep listening to what your body and Soul want. I hope you stay true to yourself above all else.

Even if at times, others' wounds try to tell you to do things their way, I hope you honor yourself. I hope you inquire, get curious and challenge what doesn't feel right. I hope you don't take others' opinions as truth, but find what feels good for YOU and create your life around it.

- my greatest wishes for my daughters, myself, and each of you

Nourish yourself with breath.
Envelope yourself with peace.
Bathe yourself with love.
Stay here. Just be.

A dream doesn't have to mean more or bigger. It can mean less. It can mean simpler. It can mean quieter.

It doesn't have to mean chasing something down. It doesn't have to mean producing anything.

A dream can be a way of living. A life based on our heart-felt yeses. A life that is quiet and calm. A life that feels good on the inside.

Slow
Simple
Spacious
Serene

They're what my dreams are made of. It's taken me a long time to realize it and get here, but each step was part of the unraveling. No end point, just continual growth and self-inquiry. Continual self-awareness and discovery. Continual honesty and acceptance.

I'm finally realizing that constant busyness doesn't work for me, but ebbs and flows do. I'm finally realizing that a job title doesn't mean I've "succeeded" or "made something of myself," but feeling at ease and peace does. I'm finally realizing that listening to my own needs in each moment is the way to live a life that's meant for me. I'm finally realizing that so much of what I used to chase, strive and hustle for, are not in alignment with my heart or soul. And the things that are, continue to reveal themselves.

Slow
Simple
Spacious
Serene
Aligned

It's important that we take time to celebrate successes that no one else notices or recognizes. The ones that are deeply personal. The shifts that even if slight, feel huge inside. One moment of everything we've been hoping for and imagining, moving in the right direction.

And when that celebratory moment slips away, may we be reminded that rather than life being a "one day at a time" journey, it actually needs to be lived "one moment at a time." Celebrating and embracing the wins, the joys, and the successes as they come. Soaking it all in. Then, taking each moment as it comes. Sometimes it feels like steps forward, sometimes like moving backward. Sometimes we feel like we're winning, and others as though we're losing. But all of it, we can choose to accept, knowing that the next moment will come - this too shall pass.

Let's celebrate as much as we can, and remember that everything changes, sometimes in the blink of an eye.

Joy is finding magic in the ordinary.

As she sat in solitude at the peak of a snowy hilltop in the wide-open prairie, surrounded by thick fog, silence and stillness, she recalled a time in her life when she prayed for *white space.*

And she took that moment to whisper a prayer of gratitude for having arrived.

Enveloped between the earth and the sky,
held,
caressed,
by the sun's shining light.

I am perfectly me,
and where I am is perfect for me.

This is what I know...
that not knowing, and letting go of trying to,
are more powerful than all the knowledge.

She didn't know she was lost

until she found herself.

Deep within my being,
a powerful force ignites,
travels up and out my crown,
into the most dazzling of sights!

Exploding like fireworks,
silver sparkles shower down,
I bask underneath,
floating on my cloud.

The feeling of BLISS,
of magic and pure joy,
childlike wonder and awe,
never to be destroyed.

I'm the dove,
I take flight,
I'm free,
My wings spread far enough for me.

   - From a powerful meditation came this sequel to my daughter's poem

acknowledgments

Every single day,

I am grateful

for little things and big things,

and things in between.

I'm grateful for the people in my life that continuously show me what it feels like to be loved, chosen and supported just for being my true self. I'm grateful for the ones who have come and gone, and all that they've taught me about myself and life.

I'm grateful for this little piece of heaven on earth that we get to call home - the rolling hills that hold peace and serenity, beauty and life; that have been my saving grace.

I'm grateful for life shifts that have brought me to where I am today and have helped me rediscover parts of myself I had forgotten.

I'm so grateful as I look around, and realize that all that I am and all that I have, I once dreamt about. I am blessed beyond measure.

Thanks for being a part of my journey, big or small, or somewhere in between.

about the author

Janelle Fettes makes her home on a ranch nestled in the rolling prairie hills of southern Saskatchewan, with her husband, two daughters, and their cattle dog, Bo. She shares her passions for wellness and compassion through yoga, meditation and reflective writing.

In a constant strive for perfection and control, Janelle spent many years struggling with eating and exercise disorders, and living in an extremely restrictive way. After welcoming her daughters into her life, she committed to her own healing in order to be a positive role model. She dove into a life-long journey of self-discovery, which led her back to her childhood love of writing.

Janelle hopes that sharing bits and pieces of her own story will help others know they are not alone in their struggles, nor their triumphs. May her words act as invitations to reconnect with yourself and as inspiration to create a life that feels good on the inside.

Manufactured by Amazon.ca
Bolton, ON